SEVEN

SECRETS

TO A

HAPPY

RETIREMENT

BY PATRICK KELLY

Cover and Interior Design by The Impact Partnership

ISBN 978-0-9833615-3-4

Printed in the USA

This book is dedicated to all those in search of a second wind, a strong finish. Know the best can be yet to come - at any age - but only if you choose it.

And also to my brother-in-law, Vince, the best family storyteller I know.

TABLE
OF
CONTENTS

PREFACE

This book captures my true heartbeat for retirement. It's the deeper message I've wanted to convey for years. A message I hope will breathe new life and new vision into your golden years ... and make them truly golden. While proper management of your money during this stage of life is foundational to a successful retirement, in the bigger perspective, there are more important factors. My hope is that these next seven chapters will give you a vision of just how powerful and exciting and adventurous your retirement years can be, as well as offer you a suggestion about the proper role money should play. Just as we seek to live by a wise adage during our working years, "Work to live ... don't live to work," I believe there's a similar principle for our retirement years, which reads something like, "Money is for living ... living is not for money."

In chapter seven, I will give you two critical and simple "must-do's" with your money to live the life described in chapters one through six, but the bulk of this book is *not* about money; rather, it's about *living*. Living a full, rewarding, exciting, inspiring, and adventurous life in retirement. The kind of life you read about in books and see in movies. The kind of life you've only dreamed of. The kind of life that is waiting for you if you're bold enough to take hold of it.

My description of retirement may look different than the one you've imagined, but I hope it's different in good ways. Different in that you can replace predictability with adventure, worry with confidence, and lethargy with vitality. So right now, before you read the pages that follow, I'm going to ask a favor of you, not for my sake, but for yours. Would you be willing, over the next few chapters, to set aside your preconceived ideas of what retirement is *supposed* to look like and open yourself up to what it *could* look like? I hope you will, because *you are worth it.*

SECRET NO. 1

DON'T RETIRE

You may think this chapter title is simply an attention grabber. It's not. I mean it. Don't retire! Don't *ever* retire!

Now before you toss this book into the nearest trash, please let me explain. I am a *huge* fan of stopping work someday, at least for the sake of earning a paycheck. However, I'm *not* a fan of stopping work altogether. I believe we were created to work, to build, to contribute. I believe work keeps us young and healthy and engaged. *But* for you to actually believe this – and live this – we first need to do two things.

One, we need to tweak your definition of "work." And two, we must dispel the falsehood that lies at the center of your current picture of retirement and expose it for the fraud it is. We all too often accept a way of life to be truth simply because *it's just the way things are* or because *everyone else is doing it*. But I find it funny how we tell our kids to guard against such dangers during their adolescent years but often fall prey to the same traps ourselves in our later years. It's a danger for all humanity – at any age. A danger I hope this chapter can help you avoid.

The falsehood that today's retirement lifestyle dishes up is the notion that our last years on this planet, the years in which we possess the most time and money and wisdom, should be filled with endless days of leisure ... on a golf course ... or a cruise ship ... or a couch. We've been fed the lie that our last two, three, or even four decades are supposed to be a never-ending weekend. A party that never stops. This is not only wrong, it's criminal. It's criminal in that it seeks to rob us of our very best years of life, the years in which we *finally* have the time and money to pursue life-long dreams. The dreams we've selflessly set aside our entire lives so we could keep food on the table and our kids in college.

Today's conventional retirement scenario may be one of the greatest thefts of talent and skill that has ever been rendered upon modern society.

It's distorted and irresponsible, and when you see how and why it came into being, it just might make you a little angry as well. Let's take a look.

By 1935, it became evident that the only way to get old people to stop working for pay was to pay them enough to stop working. A Californian, Francis Townsend, initiated a popular movement by proposing mandatory retirement at age 60. In exchange, the Government would pay pensions of up to $200 a month, an amount equivalent at the time to a full salary for a middle-income worker. Horrified at the prospect of Townsend's radical generosity, President Franklin D. Roosevelt proposed the Social Security Act of 1935, which made workers pay for their own old-age insurance.

What used to mean going to bed suddenly meant banishment to an empty stage of life called 'retirement.' If people were not going to work, what were they going to do? Sit in a rocking chair? Eleanor Roosevelt thought so. 'Old people love their own things even more than young people do. It means so much to sit in the same chair you sat in for a great many years,' she said in 1934. But she was wrong. Most retired people wished they could work. The problem was still acute in 1951, when the Corning company convened a round table to figure out how to make retirement more popular. At that conference, Santha Rama Rau, an author and student of Eastern and Western cultures, complained that Americans did not have the capacity to enjoy doing nothing.[1]

But, it goes back further than that, though its core purpose was the same. Clear out the workforce. Get rid of the old and make room for the young.

Work until you die — or until you can't work anymore. Until the late

19th century, that was the old-age plan for the bulk of the world's workers. Only in 1889 did German Chancellor Otto von Bismarck introduce modern pensions. Bismarck wasn't really motivated by compassion for the plight of the working class. He wanted to pre-empt a growing socialist movement in Germany before it grew any more powerful. ... When farming dominated the economy, most men worked as long as their health held out. As they aged, though, they often cut their hours and turned the most physically demanding chores over to sons or hired hands. In 1880, when half of Americans worked on a farm, 78 percent of American men worked past age 65.

As factories began to replace farms in economic importance, skeptics wondered whether old folks could understand and work with the new machines. One of the giants of American medicine, Johns Hopkins Hospital co-founder William Osler, in 1905 decried the 'uselessness' of men older than 60 and said they should leave the workforce. Growing prosperity also meant more people could afford to stop working late in life.

In 1875, American Express offered America's first employer-provided retirement plan. Five years later, the Baltimore and Ohio Railroad introduced the first retirement plan, financed jointly by contributions from an employer and its workers.

From there, private pension plans grew. In the United States, the plans received a boost during World War II, when the government imposed wage freezes. That led some companies to offer pensions and other benefits to attract scarce workers.

The United States created Social Security in 1935 and added Medicare health benefits for the elderly in 1965. In the 1980s, many countries lowered the age at which people could retire and collect full benefits. This step was part of an effort to clear older workers out of the labor force to make way for the young.[2]

And how did Townsend's and Bismark's plans work? Perfectly. The newly "retired" masses, who made *play* their new *work*, didn't complain one single bit, and soon the idea of retiring to a life of leisure, at age 65, was an entrenched institution.

So if retirement isn't designed to be never-ending days of leisure and relaxation, what is it supposed to be? I mean, why *wouldn't* you want to *play* for the last 30 years of your life? The answer is quite simple. The idea isn't big enough to sustain you or excite you or keep you healthy. I mean there's only so far a lower handicap or re-runs of Dr. Phil can take you.

Let me give you a couple remarkable examples of people who chose to "work" and contribute in their later years. Contributions that, if they hadn't occurred, would have left a significant void today.

I'm sure you have read at least one of Laura Ingalls Wilder's best-selling books that began with *Little House in the Big Woods.* They have been a staple in our family since I was a young boy. It was the first book series I remember my dad reading out loud when I was in grade school, and it's one we have passed on to our children as well. Did you know that Mrs. Wilder didn't publish her first book until age 64? She continued work on her series and completed it with *These Happy Golden Years* in 1943 at age 76. I'm sure you also remember the popular television series inspired by her book, which spanned from 1974 to 1982. Could you imagine the loss we'd experience if, instead of penning these words, she'd decided to simply sit in her rocking chair and sip lemonade on her front porch? She gave us a gift. A tremendous gift. A gift that allowed many of us to feel we experienced early America first-hand.

Or how about Peter Mark Roget? Does that name ring a bell? He's the author and creator of one of my favorite books — *Roget's Thesaurus.*

As Roget was nearing his 70th birthday he was forced to retire from the Royal Society, London's esteemed collection of scientists, so that the younger generation could begin its work. At that point, Roget, who was born in 1779, had done many things worthy of a secure legacy. He had developed the log-log slide rule, which allowed mathematicians to work with logarithms long before the calculator made an appearance, and he had published many medical and scientific papers, including several entries for the fledgling Encyclopedia Britannica. He was even involved with the invention of motion pictures. Instead of resting on his laurels, though, Roget turned to a project that had interested him since the time he was a young man: a scientific ordering of language. Long compelled to make lists of similar words, he envisioned a book that would not define words, but group them according to a classification. The first edition of Roget's Thesaurus was published when Roget was 73, and he oversaw every update until he died at age 90.[3]

Could you imagine if Mrs. Wilder and Mr. Roget decided their productive years were over by age 65? That they had nothing to offer? That their 60s, 70s, and 80s were going to be filled with nothing but leisure? The world would have been robbed of wonderful gifts.

The same is true for you. There is something only *you* can do. Something you were *made* to do. And once you "retire," you will finally have the time to do it. Don't miss that great gift. The world is waiting for it.

So what is Secret No. 1 for living a happy retirement? Don't retire! Plain and simple. Don't abandon yourself to the rust pile of leisure. Go work! But don't do it for pay. Do it because you love it! Do it because you *want* to! Write that book you've always pondered. Build that piece of furniture you've always imagined. Start that restaurant you've always dreamed of. Become a chef or a painter or a businesswoman. Thumb your nose at the notion (and the people) who tell you your creative and productive years have passed you by. They haven't! They have only just begun ... but only if you *choose* them. That's the *real secret* within this secret. Pursuing something significant in your life's second half doesn't just happen. It is chosen.

So what is it you want to accomplish? What is it you love to do? What is it that you've put off all of your life because there just wasn't time? What do you want to leave to the next generation or to your community? Whatever it is, make sure it's big enough, and significant enough, to give you reason to jump out of bed every morning. If you do, your mind will thank you, your body will thank you, your spouse will thank you, your children will thank you, and the generations that follow will thank you.

SECRET NO. 2

THE NEXT BIG THING

I met a car collector years ago that had amassed an amazing and rare collection of the best cars throughout history. I asked him a question I was dying to know the answer to: "Which one of these is your favorite?" I thought the question would cause him to stumble. Puzzle him for a moment. But it didn't. He said quickly, with a hint of a smirk, "The next one."

I chuckled at his answer, thinking it was mostly in jest, but quickly realized it wasn't. And I found his answer both disappointing and true. Disappointing because it displayed an enormous lack of contentment – especially with his amazing collection. However, I also recognized the truth his answer held because I understood the special anticipation and excitement that comes with *the next big thing*.

While his apparent lack of contentment was a bit sad, I do believe he gave great wisdom to all of us as it applies to our retirement years, with this one modification. I think it's dangerous to always be looking toward the *next big thing* when "*thing*" refers to a material possession. That type of behavior leads to unhappiness and discontentment. However, I think it is absolutely vital to look forward to the *next big thing* when "*thing*" is defined as a new life experience or contribution. Why is this so critical during our retirement years? Because, prior to retirement, our entire lives have been one *next big thing* after another, regardless of our choosing. There was always some *next big thing* to look forward to. Think about it. It has been true since birth.

I could give you a nauseatingly detailed list of all of the *next big things* throughout our lives, but I'll keep to a big-picture view simply to give you an idea of what I mean. Step back to your early years and march forward through the memories. As a toddler on your tricycle you yearned for the day you could sit on a big, two-wheeled bicycle and cruise freely through the neighborhood. It was the *next big thing*. When you were in grade school you anxiously awaited junior high. It was the *next big thing*. In junior high you longed for high school. It was the *next big thing*. In high school you dreamed about what lay beyond. It was the *next big thing*. In college you pictured working life. It was the *next big thing*. And during your career you strived for one promotion or raise after another. It was the *next big thing*. Somewhere along the line you likely thought about your future spouse. It was the *next big thing*. And once married, you soon pictured life with kids. It was the *next big thing*. Then if you did add children, you experienced those moments all over again as your kids lived through those same progressions.

These *next big things* seemed to never stop. And while, on one hand, there may have been times we longed for less change or for things to slow down, it was these *next big things* that kept us going, kept us excited, kept us motivated, and kept us looking forward. They kept us healthy and energized. And they still will today.

But here's the problem. Once we enter retirement, all of that changes, literally overnight. Life can stop offering us these *next big things*. They seem to slow to a crawl or even halt altogether. Think about it. School is gone. The job lies behind us. The kids are grown. And if we're not careful, we find ourselves treading a deeper and deeper rut, as our days are reduced to simple, predictable, and repetitive routines. Nothing is calling us out into the deep and exciting waters of newness and change. All of a sudden our *next big things* seem to get reduced to the next latte, the next vacation, the next dinner party, or the next sports season on television.

Don't let this happen! It doesn't need to happen. But the only way to protect against this is if you continually and actively plan your *next big thing*, because, during retirement, life will no longer be handing them to you one after another. It will be completely up to you. These next big things need to be planned and prompted – by you. They are no longer coming *at* you, but rather need to come *from* you. And while I encourage you to be content with your possessions, whether many or few, I *implore* you to *not* be content with sameness and routine. Stay hungry for your *next big thing*, at least as it relates to experiences.

And sometimes, maybe even usually, our greatest *next big things* will be ideas that seem far too lofty for us to attain. Things seemingly out of reach or beyond our talent and ability. It's these ideas that will keep us young in mind and in body.

Could you imagine what Nelson Mandela, who was sentenced by South Africa's government to life in prison at the age of 44 for his campaign against apartheid, would have said if after 28 years of being in prison was told that someday he would be the president of that same country? And what if he was also told that he wouldn't take office until he was 76 years old? I'm sure he would have quickly dismissed it as lunacy. Pure crazy talk! President? At age 76? No way! But instead it was, "Yes way!" That was simply his *next big thing*.

Or what about the author J.R.R. Tolkien? Though today he is a household name for his world-renowned trilogy, *Lord of the Rings*, I'll bet you didn't know the first volume of that trilogy wasn't written until he was 62 years old – well into the stage many are thinking about slowing down. Luckily for us, he didn't. The world was yet to receive his swan song. It was his *next big thing*.

Or let me tell you about a woman named Anna Mary Robertson Moses. A name you may not recognize, but one praised by presidents and art critics around the world.

Anna Mary Robertson Moses was better known to the world as Grandma Moses, a woman who didn't begin to paint until the age of 76, when her hands became too crippled by arthritis to hold an embroidery needle. She found herself unable to sit around and do nothing, even after a long life spent working on farms.

Grandma Moses never had any formal art training — indeed, she'd had very little formal education at all — but she painted every day, turning out more than a thousand paintings in 25 years. When an art collector passing through her town saw the paintings selling for a few dollars in a drug store, he bought them all and arranged for them to be shown at the Museum of Modern Art in New York City. ... By the time of her death, she had paintings in museums as far away as Vienna and Paris.

When Anna Mary Robertson Moses died in 1961 at age 101, then-President John F. Kennedy released a statement praising her paintings for inspiring a nation. ... Governor of New York Nelson Rockefeller had declared on her 101st birthday that there was "no more renowned artist in our entire country today."[4]

And what was all this about? It was simply her *next big thing*.

These are all people whose *next big things*, during their 60s and 70s and 80s, changed our world. But *next big things* don't have to be so lofty or as all-consuming. Your next big thing could be as simple as running (or walking) a 5K. Serving at a local food bank. Tutoring a child. Singing in a choir. Learning an instrument. Teaching a class. Taking up photography. Or traveling to a new country. Whatever it is, it's waiting out there just for you. Go find it. Go do it. Go build it. Create that list of things you want to do, big and small, a "bucket list" if you will, and then go for it!

SECRET NO. 3

FITNESS MATTERS

I've always been inspired by athletes, especially those who accomplished great feats during their later years of life. I'm not sure why they inspire me as they do. Maybe it's because I heard about so few as I was growing up. But likely it was because I dreamed of someday being such a person in my twilight years. Of doing something major and significant realm of athletic achievement or fitness. And while I've tackled a few minor things during my adult life, that thought now makes me laugh, because my midsection is currently more of a keg than a six-pack.

But I have a confession to make. Researching for and writing this book, especially this chapter, Secret No. 3, has changed me. It's prompted me to get back on the road to healthy living.

So if you feel out of shape or a little over weight, don't worry, you're not alone. But you don't have to stay there. You can live differently. You can choose a path of health and vitality. You might even do great things in the realm of fitness that you never dreamed possible. Let me tell you of such a person.

Paul E. Spangler, a retired Navy surgeon who took up running at the age of 67 to prolong his life, died on March 29, 1994 providing evidence that his theory on longevity was correct.

Dr. Spangler, whose family said he died while on one of the seven-mile runs he made three times a week near his home in San Luis Obispo, California, was 95.

In the 28 years since he began running, Dr. Spangler claimed 85 national age group records at various distances. In his last competition, in February, he won several gold medals at a senior Olympics meet in Palm Springs, Calif. By the time he began running, in 1966, Dr. Spangler had lived what many would consider a long, full life. A native of Oregon, he had served with the Navy in World War I. He had graduated from the University of Oregon and from the Harvard Medical College. He had taken up flying, becoming the first doctor, according to his family, to obtain a pilot's license. He had formed barbershop quartets all over the world, and had given long service to his country.

As a Navy doctor, he was chief of surgery at the base hospital near Pearl Harbor on Dec. 7, 1941, and after he retired as a captain in 1959, he served as chief medical officer aboard the hospital ship Hope on a 1960 tour of southeast Asia. After that, he was a surgeon at the California Men's Colony, a state prison in San Luis Obispo. Dr. Spangler was chairman of his chapter of the American Heart Association when he realized that being a weekend athlete, playing tennis, climbing mountains and digging clams, was not enough to stave off heart disease.

Running became his career. "Running has meant everything to me," he said before competing in the 1989 New York City Marathon at the age of 90. "My only mission in life now is to convince people this is possible. With proper living, they can eliminate coronary heart disease."[5]

That's not too shabby for a man who didn't begin running until he was 67 years old. And why did he do it? Because during his years as a surgeon he saw the devastating effects on a body without regular exercise. So he went for it and made headlines in the process.

What is it you like to do? Walk, run, hike, bicycle, paddle, play tennis or golf? Whatever it is, get out there and do it. And maybe, just maybe, you might just surprise yourself.

I'll bet you've never heard of a lady named Barbara Hillary. I hadn't. But I don't understand how that can be. She is a remarkable woman. A woman to inspire us all. She not only beat a five-year battle against lung cancer, beginning at age 67, which is a great victory in itself, but at the age of 75 she was one the oldest people on record, and the first black woman, to reach the North Pole. Here's a great article about her accomplishment from the May 7, 2007, edition of *The Seattle Times*.

The bone-numbing trek to the North Pole is riddled with enough perils to make a seasoned explorer quake: frostbite threatens, polar bears loom and the ice is constantly shifting beneath frozen feet.

But Barbara Hillary took it all in stride, completing the trek to the world's northernmost point last month at the age of 75. She is one of the oldest people to reach the North Pole, and is believed to be the first black woman to accomplish the feat.

Hillary, of Averne, N.Y., grew up in Harlem and devoted herself to a nursing career and community activism. At 67, she battled lung cancer. Five years later, she went dog sledding in Quebec and photographed polar bears in Manitoba.

Then she heard that a black woman had never made it to the North Pole.

"What's wrong with this picture?" she said. "So I sort of rolled into this, shall we say." ... Hillary insisted on skiing. Only trouble was, she had never been on skis before.

"It wasn't a popular sport in Harlem," she quipped.

So she enrolled in cross-country-skiing lessons and hired a personal trainer, who finally determined she was physically fit for the voyage. ... Her lack of money didn't stop her, either. Hillary scraped together thousands of dollars and solicited private donors.[6]

But Mrs. Hillary's adventures didn't stop there. Four years after that record-breaking trek to the North Pole she decided to conquer the south end of the globe as well. An article printed in the March 11, 2011, edition of The New York Post is so inspiring I had to share it with you as well.

She made it into the record books by reaching the top of the planet in 2007 — and this year, at age 79, Queens cancer survivor and trailblazer Barbara Hillary historically made the trek to the bottom too.

"Barbara, you finally did it," the retired, Harlem-born nurse recalled thinking as she stood at the South Pole on Jan. 31, fewer than four years after mastering the North Pole. "Or maybe I died and went to the great expedition in the sky!"

Hillary became the first black woman to go to either pole, much less both.

"I refuse to get older and be boring to myself and others," she told The Post.

In her latest venture, Hillary said, she braved four nights with 25-below-zero temperatures in an unheated tent after bad weather delayed the expedition's propeller-plane departure from a base camp at the South Pole.

"At the time, I was thinking I could be in a comfortable bed, watching television and enjoying a nice cup of tea," said Hillary, a breast- and lung-cancer survivor.

Her $40,000 trip had taken a month to complete because of repeated weather delays. She had already spent a year on trip preparations, which included near-daily fund-raising calls to outdoor-gear and other companies to sponsor the adventure.

"I'm on a fixed income: Where else would I get the money?" she asked.

Yet even the stark beauty of the North Pole in 2007 didn't prepare Hillary for the exquisite Antarctic, she said. Hillary noted that the land-

scape was a wonder of huge white mountains and shifting blue-gray shadows that responded to the sun circling the sky — and her excitement at being there made it hard to heed the advice of the expedition's doctor, who warned her about the thin air at 9,300 feet above sea level.

"The doctor said walk slowly, very slowly, but I was on an emotional and physical roller coaster," she confessed.

Hillary said she came to exploration late in life — venturing to photograph polar bears in Manitoba, Canada, for her first post-retirement adventure.

"I fell in love with the beauty of nature and the chance to meet free-thinking, dynamic people who had an excitement for life," said Hillary, who never married.

"When some people get to 65, they start to shuffle," Hillary said. "They say they can't move that fast. I tell them to walk briskly."

"The old saying 'Use it, or lose it,' is true."[7]

I don't know how you feel after reading that, but I am inspired. Inspired by a 75-year old woman's determination to make her golden years spectacular. Inspired (and humbled) by feats of athleticism by a woman 30 years my senior that put me to shame. Inspired that a nurse from the city had the vision to battle and overcome every obstacle that stood in her way to accomplish something great — and virtually everything stood in her way.

Think about it. She didn't know how to ski. She didn't have the money. She had only recently conquered a life-threatening battle against cancer. And I'm certain she was told by everyone who knew her that she was crazy, that she might injure herself or even die, and that it simply couldn't be done by a woman of her age — because it hadn't been done by a woman of her age. Everything was against her. But she stepped up and did it. And she's still going strong.

But you know what? There are Barbaras all around us. You may even be a Barbara. And if you're not yet, you can be. I recently met such a Barbara flying home from taking our second oldest to college. My wife and I arrived at the airport just before our flight took off and by the time we boarded the plane the only two seats left were two middle seats across the aisle from one another. But this small inconvenience allowed me to meet someone I otherwise wouldn't have had the privilege of meeting.

This lady, who appeared to be in her early 70s, was heading to Vancouver, B.C., for two weeks of badminton coaching to prepare for the World Master Games in Auckland, New Zealand, in 2017. She didn't look like an athlete. She looked just like any other 70-year-old woman, except for the youthful twinkle in her eye. She told me she decided she wanted to be more active in her later years, so she took time to ponder what sport she might enjoy. She had played some badminton in college but hadn't played it for nearly 50 years but decided it was the one. So she got serious. Took a few lessons. And started competing in senior tournaments around the country.

You could see the smile creases as she told me she'd even won a couple of national tournaments. She was proud. And had every right to be. I was proud of her and I didn't even know her. But I was proud to see someone going for it in her 70s, not settling for what the world was telling her she could or couldn't do. And though she admitted that her body didn't heal from injury quite as quickly as it used to, she said she felt younger than she had in decades. And it showed.

In my research for this chapter, I read one amazing story after another. And I wish I had the space to share them all. Like Yuichiro Miura, the 80-year-old Japanese man who became the oldest person to reach the summit of Mount Everest. Or 84-year-old Bill Painter, who reached the summit of Mount Rainier for the sixth time, his first summit coming at age 76. Or Teiichi Igarashi, who climbed Mount Fuji at age 99. Or a man named Frank Schearerwho was still water skiing at age 100. These are all amazing individuals with amazing stories.

Your story can be amazing, too. And you don't need to book a trip to Nepal or ski your way to the North Pole to make it so. I simply tell you these stories because I want you to see what is possible so you can begin to expand your perspective and horizon of what you can accomplish during your retirement years. For you, it might be quite simple. No headlines or pomp and circumstance. Just a simple plan – like joining a gym and actually going, or buying a bike and actually riding, or signing up for a race and actually training.

If you're like most of us, though, you are battling two enemies who are eagerly trying to keep you fat, lazy, and on the couch. The first of these enemies is Mr. Inertia. Mr. Inertia makes that first step so heavy and so ominous that it's simply easier not to attempt. But Mr. Inertia is forced to loosen his grip just by the act of lacing up our running shoes. If we just do it. Move forward. Go for it. He's forced to let go. His grip is broken by our action. So whether it's starting with a slow walk around the block or a longer run around the community, whatever it is – get out there and do it.

Our second enemy is Mr. Discouragement. He whispers things in our ear like, "Ha! You? Lose weight? Why didn't you think about that 10 years ago? You're far too fat to ever get back into shape." And, unfortunately, we listen. And by listening, instead of reversing the effects of weight and age and a sedentary life, we simply continue our waltz down the easy road of decay and disease. We throw in the proverbial towel before we ever begin, deciding it's easier, and far more pleasant, to keep the running shoes in the closet and opt for cocktail hour. But you know as well as I do, though too often we don't want to admit it to ourselves or it might mean we'll have to sweat, that this road often leads to diabetes and obesity, and eventually an early death.

Sorry, that came across a bit heavy-handed, but sometimes we need a little discomfort before we are willing to make a change. And sometimes the truth stings. But it's better for my words to cause you a little unease than the pain of a blocked artery and a triple bypass.

We all know staying active will keep us healthier, but often that knowledge doesn't translate into action. That is the key. Do something! I could pepper you with myriad articles I read about how aerobic exercise offsets not only heart disease but cognitive impairment (dementia) as well, not to mention a host of other diseases. But you already know this. Lack of knowledge isn't the problem; action is.

It's not unlike the writing of a book. At least for me. I have an idea. I have a plan. I have an end-goal in mind. But unless I force myself to sit and actually write consistently every week, without fail, the book will never graduate from simply an idea. It just sits there. Unrealized potential.

So today you need to choose. What do you want your last decades on this earth to look like? Oxygen tubes at a slot machine or digging your ice pick on the summit of Mount Everest?

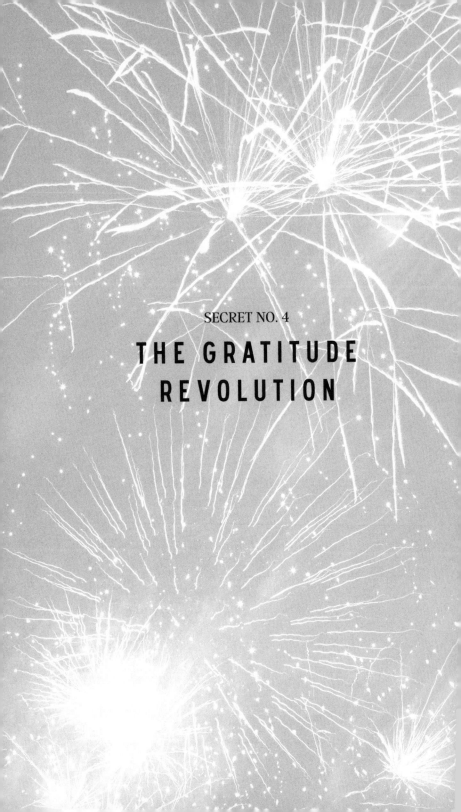

SECRET NO. 4

THE GRATITUDE
REVOLUTION

If you knew — I mean really *knew* — you could extend your life by doing one simple thing, something you were guaranteed to be able to accomplish with ease (and wouldn't make you sweat) would you do it? Before you say, "Yes," too quickly, think about it. Are you sure? Because if you are, then read this chapter carefully, because Secret No. 4 will do just that and is both easily achievable by everyone as well as scientifically *proven* not only to extend the length of your life but its quality as well.

What is this life-giving secret? Gratitude. Simply the act (and attitude) of being grateful.

I must admit that I struggled with the title of this chapter a bit, because, currently, I don't believe there *is* a Gratitude Revolution. But I want there to be one. So I kept it with the hope that these pages might be part of the genesis of such a revolution. A revolution that might offer joy and health to all who are willing to participate.

As I thought through and planned the "Seven Secrets" I believed would most significantly contribute to a happy and fulfilling retirement, gratitude was on every list. I knew it *had* to be, because the happiest people I've known in their later years all shared one trait — an attitude of gratitude. What I didn't expect, however, was just how much medical and scientific study had been done on the subject. I was shocked. While my non-scientific observation showed evidence, the scientific and medical data is irrefutable. Take a look.

In a WebMD article titled "Boost Your Health With a Dose of Gratitude: If You Want to Get Healthier, Give Thanks," Elizabeth Heubeck writes:

Can just a positive emotion such as gratitude guarantee better health?
It may be a dramatic departure from what we've been taught about how

to get healthier, but the connection between gratitude and health actually goes back a long way.

"Thousands of years of literature talk about the benefits of cultivating gratefulness as a virtue," says University of California Davis psychology professor Robert Emmons. Throughout history, philosophers and religious leaders have extolled gratitude as a virtue integral to health and well-being. Now, through a recent movement called positive psychology, mental health professionals are taking a close look at how virtues such as gratitude can benefit our health. And they're reaping some promising results.

Grateful people — those who perceive gratitude as a permanent trait rather than a temporary state of mind — have an edge on the not-so-grateful when it comes to health, according to Emmons' research on gratitude. "Grateful people take better care of themselves and engage in more protective health behaviors like regular exercise, a healthy diet, and regular physical examinations," Emmons tells WebMD.

It's no secret that stress can make us sick, particularly when we can't cope with it. It's linked to several leading causes of death, including heart disease and cancer, and claims responsibility for up to 90% of all doctor visits. Gratitude, it turns out, can help us better manage stress. "Gratitude research is beginning to suggest that feelings of thankfulness have tremendous positive value in helping people cope with daily problems, especially stress," Emmons says.

Grateful people tend to be more optimistic, a characteristic that researchers say boosts the immune system. "There are some very interesting studies linking optimism to better immune function," says Lisa Aspinwall, PhD, a psychology professor at the University of Utah. In one, researchers comparing the immune systems of healthy, first-year law students under stress found that, by midterm, students characterized as optimistic (based on survey responses) maintained higher numbers of blood cells that protect the immune system, compared with their more pessimistic classmates.

Optimism also has a positive health impact on people with compromised health. In separate studies, patients confronting AIDS, as well as those preparing to undergo surgery, had better health outcomes when they maintained attitudes of optimism.[8]

In an article called "The 31 Benefits of Gratitude You Didn't Know About: How Gratitude Can Change Your Life," the author, Amit Amin, reveals 31 benefits by combining and aggregating the results of more than 40 research studies on gratitude. In his very first benefit, *Gratitude makes us happier,* Amin says, "*A five-minute a day gratitude journal can increase your long-term well-being by more than 10 percent. That's the same impact as doubling your income!*"[9]

Think about that! That's incredibly significant.

In Amin's benefit number three, *Gratitude makes us happier,* he gives us this compelling research from various studies:[10]

RESULTS	STUDY	YEAR
Keeping a gratitude journal caused participants to report **16% fewer physical symptoms, 19% more time spent exercising 10% less physical pain, 8% more sleep, and 25% increased sleep quality**	Counting Blessings Versus Burdens	2003
The emotions of appreciation and gratitude shown to induce the relaxation response.	The Grateful Heart	2004

A gratitude visit **reduced depressive symptoms by 35% for several weeks;** a gratitude journal **lowered depressive symptoms by 30%+ for as long as the practice was continued.**	Positive Psychology Progress	2005
Patients with hypertension were instructed to count their blessings once a week. There was a **significant decrease in their systolic blood pressure.**	Gratitude: Effects on Perspectives and Blood Pressure	2007
Gratitude correlated with **improved sleep quality** (r=.29), **less time required to fall asleep** (r=.20), **and increased sleep duration** (r=.14).	Gratitude Influences Sleep Through the Mechanism of Pre-Sleep Cognitions	2009
Levels of gratitude significantly correlated with **vitality and energy.**	Multiple Studies	Many

This may be why the Greater Good Science Center at the University of California, Berkeley – in collaboration with the University of California, Davis – launched a $5.6 million, three-year project, Expanding the Science and Practice of Gratitude.[11]

And lastly, an article in *Harvard Health Publications* by the Harvard Medical School titled "In Praise of Gratitude," reads:

Two psychologists, Dr. Robert A. Emmons of the University of California, Davis, and Dr. Michael E. McCullough of the University of Miami, have done much of the research on gratitude. In one study, they asked all participants to write a few sentences each week, focusing on particular topics.

One group wrote about things they were grateful for that had oc-

curred during the week. A second group wrote about daily irritations or things that had displeased them, and the third wrote about events that had affected them (with no emphasis on them being positive or negative). After 10 weeks, those who wrote about gratitude were more optimistic and felt better about their lives. Surprisingly, they also exercised more and had fewer visits to physicians than those who focused on sources of aggravation. ...Of course, studies such as this one cannot prove cause and effect. But most of the studies published on this topic support an association between gratitude and an individual's well-being.

Other studies have looked at how gratitude can improve relationships. For example, a study of couples found that individuals who took time to express gratitude for their partner not only felt more positive toward the other person but also felt more comfortable expressing concerns about their relationship.[12]

Gratitude can take different forms. One form I witnessed during my early years was displayed by my grandmother. I'm not sure a more grateful person has ever walked this earth. And this isn't just the naive perspective of a grandson; it is corroborated by everyone who knew her. Grateful, content, and happy would be three adjectives that perfectly described her. But I believe her contentment and happiness stemmed from her attitude of gratefulness. And it wasn't portrayed through grandiose displays or verbose monologues. Rather, her contentment was lived and displayed each and every moment of her life, regardless of what she was doing.

As a child, one day I watched her working in the kitchen, humming and smiling.

"Grandma, why are you so happy?" I asked. "You're just peeling potatoes."

She paused, turned to me, and said, "It's just so wonderful to be alive, Patrick. I am so blessed to get to do all the wonderful things I do. I love absolutely everything. Even peeling potatoes."

I'm not exaggerating. That is what she said. Maybe not word for word, as it was over 30 years ago, but that was what she told me, and that message has been embedded deeply on my psyche since that day. I have reflected back on it many times, as I've been tempted to complain or feel sorry for myself because things hadn't gone as planned. And just to be clear on one thing, don't for a minute think she was able to live this joyful and grateful attitude simply because her life had been easy and trouble-free. She lived a life full of difficulties and challenges, beginning at the young age of 10 when her mother died of scarlet fever because she had cared for a sick neighbor girl. My grandmother, as an only child, lost her mother and her best friend. And life kept tossing challenges her way.

But instead of letting those events taint her perspective, and make her grouchy and negative, she chose gratitude – every hour of every day. And that simple choice made her one of the most exceptional individuals I've ever met. And also allowed her to live to the wonderful age of 92.

Right now you may be dealing with any number of different challenges, all of varying degrees. On the significant side, maybe it's a health issue you've been wrestling with for years. Or maybe it's one that's just been diagnosed. If so, be grateful for life *today*. Give thanks for the things you get to do *today*. Even if it's as simple as peeling potatoes.

Or maybe you're struggling through estrangement with children or a family member or a long-time friend. That can be excruciatingly difficult and not always within your ability to change. Try this. Give thanks for that person. Be thankful for him or her. Write a short note expressing all the things you appreciate about them and how much you value your relationship. But it must be sincere, and it can't contain any element that might produce guilt. I'm sure you know what I mean.

Or maybe your challenge right now might be a step less significant than those other two, like possessing a smaller savings account than you planned for retirement. Or feeling the aches and pains begin to set in. Or needing to work when you'd like to retire. Or any number of infinitely different things.

I can't guarantee you many things in life, but I *can* guarantee you this – life is full of challenge after challenge, and difficulty after difficulty. That's our only guarantee. This life will be full of trials. Some more significant than others. So Secret No. 4 to living a happy retirement is not – I repeat *not* – about trying to get to a point in life in which you have eliminated the struggles and challenges; rather, secret No. 4 for living a happy retirement is to show gratitude toward, and be thankful for, every person and every experience – every day.

SECRET NO. 5

SHARE YOUR
STORIES

My grandfather on my mother's side was the youngest of nine. He was a tease. An adventurer. A tough and scrappy little guy. And more often than not, he had his nose right in the middle of a heap of mischief, at least during most of his youth. But that's *exactly* what made his stories so marvelous.

He was born in 1913 in rural Arizona. Actually "rural" is an overstatement. His closest neighbor lived six miles away. There were seven kids in his entire school (not class, but school), and four of them were his brothers and sisters. And if there was one thing my grandfather could do, he could tell a great story.

When I was 12, he told me a story that I was convinced was the fish story to end all fish stories. We've all heard them, haven't we? The one that got away. The minnow that became a whale two hours after it was caught. And I was sure this story was just that — the ultimate fish yarn — as he told me about the giant halibut he caught in Alaska during his time in the Coast Guard...off the end of a dock...on a line wrapped around his hand. Here's how it went:

"We were stationed in Alaska and had just come into port. I wanted to go fishing, but I had two problems. One, I didn't have a boat. And two, I didn't have a pole. But I decided to go fishing anyway. I grabbed some line, a hook, and some bait, and I walked to the end of the dock our boat had just tied to and dropped a line in the water. And wouldn't you know, within about an hour, I had a monster halibut on the end of my line."

"No way!" I said, my 12-year-old skepticism on red-alert. "There's no way you caught a fish with your bare hands off the end of a dock."

"As a matter of fact, I did. And not just any fish, Patrick. A monster. A 163-pound halibut."

"Seriously? Are you making this up or did it really happen?"

"This is as real as the nose on your face," my grandpa said.

"How'd you get it in?" I asked.

"Well, after about four hours of slowly looping the line around and around my hand, I was starting to lose circulation, and my hand was cut to shreds, so I whistled at someone on the ship to get me a glove."

"No way!" I said again, my disbelief continuing to build. "You hauled up a 163-pound halibut with your bare hands?"

"Yep. Sure did. But boy that glove really helped."

I chuckled at the understatement. "Okay, so how'd you get it up on the dock?"

"Well, after the sailor who brought me the glove went back aboard the ship, he told the crew what I was doing. Soon I had an audience on the deck of the ship watching from above. They were cheering and yelling. Whooping and hollering. And when I finally got that big fish to the surface, they lowered the Coast Guard crane to haul that monster up onto the ship's deck. And you know the best part?"

"What?"

"It fed the entire Coast Guard ship that night – every single one of us – with fish to spare."

"Wow, Grandpa. That could be the greatest fish story I've ever heard. I wish I could have seen that guy."

"Well, as a matter of fact, I think you can," he said. "I believe I have a picture around here somewhere in one of these old photo albums."

And sure enough, he did. And any lingering skepticism immediately vanished as he dug out the album and showed me that magnificent, black and white picture of him standing on the end of that dock with a virtual whale hanging next to him by its tail.

Wow. What a story. But that wasn't his only one. He had dozens.

Like the time when he was 6, barefoot in the Arizona desert, tending the family's small flock of sheep. He came across a rattlesnake that he feared might hurt the animals in his care. And he did what every normal 6-year-old would do. He took the shovel he was carrying and chopped that rattlesnake's head clean off. At 6! I could barely read a book or ride a bike at 6. And my grandpa was tending the family's prized flock and killing rattlesnakes with a shovel.

Or, like the time when he stowed aboard a passing freight train from Seattle all the way to Los Angeles to see the 1932 Summer Olympics. It's a classic. During the day he'd climb on top of the boxcars and lay spread eagle, both to hold on and so he wouldn't be seen. At night, he'd climb down between two of the cars and loop his belt around one of the metal poles holding the cars together. He said it was the only way he could sleep without falling off during the night. Think about that. Today most of us complain about the lack of leg room in coach class; and here's my grandpa sleeping standing up, looped onto a moving freight train by a two-inch piece of worn leather. How crazy. How cool. And this is *my* bloodline.

Or, like the time, or should I say *times,* when he and his brothers burned their family's house to the ground...two Fourth of Julys in a row. Yes, complete and total loss, two years in a row. Both times because he and his brothers threw firecrackers in the air that landed on their dry Arizona roof. How terrible. How amazing. And this is part of *my* history. The stories continued, and I loved every one. I could sit for hours and just listen. And through the years I did exactly that. I so wish I'd recorded them, not only to hear those marvelous exploits again and again, but also to hear the joy in my grandpa's voice as he told them.

I loved Hardenbrook family reunions, especially when my grandpa and all eight of his brothers and sisters were alive. There were hundreds of us in attendance, spanning four generations. We'd all gather around at the end of the first day and listen to new stories and old. One by one they'd pass the microphone, and we'd sit and watch the memories reengage after decades. Feeding off of each other. Reminiscing together.

I remember thinking. Wow. This is *my* lineage. *My* heritage. *My* family.

And now they're gone. All of them. None of the nine are still with us – but their stories are. The stories will live forever. Stories of moving and homesteading, of building careers and failed businesses, of raising kids and losing loved ones ... and on and on and on. They were the stories of our family. The stories of our lives, both individual and corporate.

And now as I look back, I think *this* is wealth. *This* is how legacies are built and families are bonded. *This* is what life is really about. Inheriting money may be nice, but inheriting stories is sacred. So why do I tell you this? Simple. Secret No. 5 to living a happy retirement is this: Tell your stories. Tell them all. Tell your children. Tell your grandchildren. Tell them what life was like when you were their age. Tell them your greatest adventure as a teenager. Tell them how you met their grandmother or grandfather. Tell them your biggest failure. Your biggest regret. Tell them about the time you were most excited or about your greatest success. Tell them everything. They want to hear it. All of it.

Trust me. If you make the time, they'll want to listen. And they'll remember everything you tell them. And it will be these stories that will live on in your family's heritage for generations to come. Remember, with all of the effort you put into planning, with all of your desire to leave a financial legacy when your time on earth is done, don't forget to give your family one of the most valuable gifts of all – your stories.

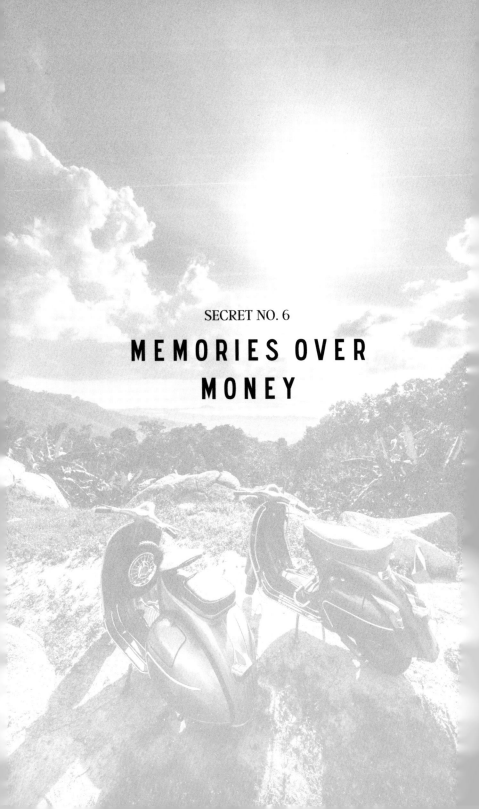

SECRET NO. 6

MEMORIES OVER MONEY

Decades ago, when my grandmother was still alive, I overheard her mention that she and her step-sister had finally reconciled after 50 years of total and complete estrangement. Fifty years! Can you believe that? Unfortunately, it happens all the time; yet many (maybe most) don't have a happy ending. Fortunately, for my grandmother, hers did. She and her step-sister entered eternity as the best of friends. Unfortunately, neither of them could do anything to make up for all of those lost years. Years that would have added meaning and texture to both of their lives.

And you'll never guess what started this half-century dispute. A set of china. (Yes, as in dishes.) It's a long story, as it usually is. But, in short, this dispute originated with "STUFF." While that seems totally ridiculous to me, I fear it's far too common.

I remember playing golf a few years ago with a couple of guys I didn't know. As we hacked around the course together, one of them shared with me his perspective on "stuff."

He said, "I don't care that much about stuff. The way I see it, the only things we can take with us when we die are our memories and our relationships."

Wow. Good words. As a matter of fact, I think memories and relationships just may be the currency of eternity.

But if that really is the case, then why do most people spend their lives acting like it's all of their "stuff" that matters most? Their money. Their things. The last time I checked, "stuff" *always* gets left behind. As the old adage goes, "You never see a hearse pulling a U-Haul."

So, if we can't bring it with us, what *should* we do with it? How should we use our money and our things? Those are deeply important questions. Questions we often contemplate too late in life, just as the twilight is fading to darkness.

However, I want to help you think through this right now, while you still have all of your options. And I'm going to propose to you that the highest calling for your stuff, its greatest purpose, is to use it to build those two precious things that *do* last forever — memories and relationships.

How can you do this? I think you inherently know; but just in case, I'll make it absolutely clear. Spend it. Not wastefully or frivolously. Not in a way that puts your living expenses in jeopardy. But, rather, spend it in a way that maximizes all of that extra money, all of the "stuff" that is going to get left behind, in such a way as to bless those you love and build special memories that you will all carry into eternity. Isn't that what we really want? To be remembered with fondness. To know we made a difference in the lives of others and left our mark. That is secret No. 6.

For example, instead of stockpiling that extra $15,000 or $20,000 in some sterile and impersonal bank account, take your children and grandchildren — your entire gaggle of offspring — on a cruise. Let them experience a part of the world they would never otherwise see. Enjoy dining together each night with a view of the vast Pacific. Explore ancient cultures as you hold your 8-year-old granddaughter's hand. Show them what a "cool" 70-year-old grandmother looks like as you zip-line through the treetops of Costa Rica. Or fish the majestic rivers of Canada. Think about all the things you could do. Take them to see Mickey Mouse. Or a sunrise in the Greek Isles. Or the Northern Lights in Alaska. Think about all of those incredible memories. Isn't that infinitely more valuable than leaving them money? Doesn't that make your heart sing just a little louder?

And it can be even more significant than that. Your "stuff" can create blessings far beyond just your own family. Think what a blessing your money could be for those who are literally thirsting and starving to death around the world. For those whose lives are being devastated by natural disasters and human atrocities. Individuals you may never know but can certainly bless.

Doesn't that get your blood pumping just a little faster? To know that you used whatever you had, whether it was a little or a lot, to be a blessing to others? I can't think of a higher calling for our finances or many greater joys.

And think about this. If we consider individuals wise who invest their money for 30 or 40 years, how much more wisdom would we assign to individuals who invest for eternity? Who build a storehouse of memories and relationships that will last forever? Who give to those who would otherwise perish? Now that's the kind of investment I want to make.

And think how amusing it would be if, as you're crossing the finish line of life, you had planned so well and spent so lavishly on others that the last check you wrote, the one to the undertaker, actually bounced. Ha. How fun would that be? I'll bet your kids would double over with laughter knowing that you invested everything into building memories with them and their children. Who knows? Maybe they'd even be willing to write the check to get you buried.

OK, while that last thought is clearly an exaggeration for the sake of humor, I'm sure you get the picture. Don't stress about spending the money you've saved. That's exactly what it's for. Give it. Spend it. And use it to make a difference in the lives of others and to create a life full of blessed memories and relationships. If you do, I can most certainly guarantee you one thing – a life well lived.

SECRET NO. 7

FINANCIAL AUTOPILOT

I hope by now you realize that retirement is about a *lot* more than money. It's about life. About living that life to the fullest measure possible and leaving behind stories and ideas and creations that will continue on for generations. But even though money takes a back seat in importance to all of the other secrets we have discussed in this book, it's still a *significant* part of our lives, especially once the consistent income from our career or profession has ceased.

It's simple psychology, really. Not unlike the "hierarchy of needs" proposed by Abraham Maslow in his 1943 paper "A Theory of Human Motivation" in *Psychological Review*.[13] In brief summary, Maslow's theory says that people can't (or won't) focus on self-actualization needs, such as creativity and potential, until their fundamental physical and safety needs are met. This makes perfect sense. If someone is hungry or feels threatened, it's unlikely he will be pondering the next mountain he wants to climb. His sole focus is his next meal.

I believe – strongly believe – a similar hierarchy of needs exists in our financial lives as well, though I've never heard anyone speak about it in those terms. I'm not talking about portfolio management or risk allocation; I'm talking about something much more fundamental.

If people are forced to spend time and effort worrying about their money – whether they will have enough to pay their bills this month or whether their nest egg will last their entire lives – they *cannot* be sufficiently freed up to fully pursue and live out Secrets No. 1 through No. 6 in this book. The "money fear," whether subtle or immense, will keep them blocked at the base of the hierarchy pyramid, not allowing them to reach the top, both figuratively and literally.

Just like Maslow says that we can't focus on our self-actualization desires until our fundamental needs are met, I say we can't free ourselves up to live a full and rich and significant life of contribution and accomplishment until we release our fear-based questions of: *Is my money safe? Will my money last? Is my money in the right place?*

If you are in (or near) retirement, you likely can't change the amount of money you have currently saved; however, you *can* determine how much you *keep.* That should be your top priority. Keep what you've saved! Protect the money you've worked so hard to accumulate. You've spent your entire working life accumulating it. Don't give it all back in a heartbeat due to market forces you can't control or predict. Taking that risk may be tolerable during your working years because you have time to recover, time to keep saving. But once the income stops, everything changes. Or at least everything *should* change. And the number one thing that *should* change is removing any potential risk of loss. Get rid of it! Completely! It stands to do more damage to your financial well-being than any other variable I can think of. It will also be the issue that keeps you up at night and prevents you from freely pursuing your *next big thing* and the vibrant life described earlier in this book.

So *part one* of Secret No. 7 is this — have a strategy that aims to *remove the potential for loss from your portfolio.*

You might be thinking, "Sure, anyone can do that. All they need to do is stick their money under the mattress or in a tin can in the back yard, and they won't lose a cent. But that's not a good recipe for making money either. And that's just as dangerous."

And I'd agree. But here's the thing. Just because your strategy aims to remove the potential for loss doesn't mean you need to give up the opportunity for gain. And that's not only great news, it's also *part two* of Secret No. 7 — while you protect yourself against loss, *don't give up the opportunity for growth.* Significant growth. And fortunately, that can be possible with today's financial offerings.

As a matter of fact, I've made it one of my life's missions over the last decade to help people do just that. To tell the masses that, in today's financial world, there are ways to protect against losing money due to market corrections without giving up the possibility for growth when the market has a positive year.

No, that is not too good to be true; it is simply a more modern portfolio management style. Something that is remarkably easy to accomplish, though not something you often hear spoken of ... except by the very well informed.

And that is *part three* of Secret No. 7 — *work with a professional who is fully informed on how to accomplish parts one and two.* In other words, work with someone who knows how to help protect you against taking another loss. Someone who can show you options that offer protection against the market's downside, while at the same time, does not force you to give up the potential for gain. That strategy *does* exist. As a matter of fact, hundreds of thousands of individuals are taking advantage of it. *

So why don't you make sure you are one of those individuals? Luckily, that might be very easy to do. The answer might be just a phone call away. As a matter of fact, if a financial professional gave you this book, it is likely because he or she is in the business of helping people accomplish this very goal — protecting what they've accumulated without giving up the opportunity for growth. If that is the case, do yourself a favor and schedule a visit. They can likely show you just how easy it is to accomplish. And you know what? Those few minutes might just be the best financial decision you ever make, as well as your *next big thing!*

---

* These types of strategies exist because they rely upon insurance contract guarantees that

apply to certain insurance and annuity products (not securities, variable or investment advisory products) including optional benefits, and are subject to product terms, exclusions and limitations as well as the insurer's claims-paying ability and the financial strength of the issuing insurance company.

ENDNOTES

[1] Mary Lou Weisman, "The History of Retirement, From Early Man to A.A.R.P.," The New York Times, March 21, 1999.

[2] "A brief history of retirement: It's a modern idea," The Seattle Times, December 31, 2013.

[3] "10 Famous Accomplishments Made Late in Life," http://health.howstuffworks.com/wellness/aging/senior-health-lifestyle/5-famous-accomplishments-made-late-in-life.htm

[4] "10 Famous Accomplishments Made Late in Life"

[5] Robert McG. Thomas Jr., "Dr. Paul E. Spangler, 95, Dies; Took Up Fitness Running at 67," The New York Times, April 14, 1994.

[6] Meghan Barr, "75-year-old cancer survivor skis to North Pole," The Seattle Times, May 7, 2007.

[7] Len Maniace, "She's bi-'Polar,'" The New York Post, March 11, 2011.

[8] "Boost Your Health With a Dose of Gratitude," http://www.webmd.com/women/features/gratitute-health-boost?page=2

[9] "The 31 Benefits of Gratitude You Didn't Know About: How Gratitude Can Change Your Life," http://happierhuman.com/benefits-of-gratitude/

[10] "The 31 Benefits of Gratitude You Didn't Know About: How Gratitude Can Change Your Life"

[11] "Expanding the Science and Practice of Gratitude," http://greatergood.berkeley.edu/expandinggratitude

[12] "In Praise of Gratitude," http://www.health.harvard.edu/newsletter_article/in-praise-of-gratitude

[13] A.H. Maslow, "A Theory of Human Motivation," Psychological Review Vol. 50(4) (1943) 370-96

Patrick Kelly is the author of four national best-selling books, *Tax-Free Retirement* (2007), *The Retirement Miracle* (2011), *Stress-Free Retirement* (2013), and *The 5 Retirement Myths* (2015) which together have sold more than 1.5 million copies. Patrick has spent much of his career on a national platform delivering his unique message to over 100,000 advisors from coast to coast and has become one of the industry's most sought-after speakers. Patrick's strong counsel for advisors to practice an ethical, "client first" philosophy is the centerpiece of all his messages. One of his greatest passions is to help consumers understand they are able to step off the roller coaster of fear and loss and onto the peace-filled road of growth and stability.